MW01153083

Calm and Peaceful
Mindful Me

A Mindfulness How-to Guide
for Toddlers and Kids

Andrea Dorn, MSW

Calm and Peaceful Mindful Me
Copyright © 2021 Andrea Dorn

Published by:
PESI Publishing & Media
PESI, Inc.
3839 White Ave.
Eau Claire, WI 54703

Illustrations: Andrea Dorn
Cover: Andrea Dorn
Layout: Andrea Dorn & Amy Rubenzer
ISBN: 9781683733744

All rights reserved
Printed in Canada

PESI Publishing
pesipublishing.com

Dedication

For Henry and William,
my greatest teachers,
inspirators, and joy bringers

Oh! Hi there! What is your name?

Really?! That is MY name too!

I am growing every day, and as I grow,
I get to learn lots of fun things!

Optional question: What fun things do you know how to do?

Sometimes all that learning makes my brain and body feel VERY busy and VERY full, so one fun thing I am learning is how to use mindfulness to help me have a calm and peaceful body and mind.

Optional questions: What makes your brain and body feel busy and full? What do you think mindfulness is?

Mindfulness is when I stop to pay attention
to my body and my heart and when I notice things
around me just as they are **right now.**

When I stop to notice what's happening right now,
my body has more room for peaceful
thoughts and peaceful feelings.
I know my body is peaceful when it is quiet,
kind, still, and does good listening.

Optional question: Who has a calm and
peaceful body where you are right now?

Here is how I practice mindfulness.

First, I stop what I am doing and take a deep belly breath to slow my body down.

(I can speed it up again later!)

I can take a deep belly breath by pretending my tummy is a big balloon:

I breathe in and blow up my belly balloon.

Then I let the air out of my balloon as I breathe out and relax my body.

Optional questions: What color is your balloon? How big can you make your belly balloon? (For older children, practice noticing the sensations of your breathing as the air fills and then leaves your body.) What does it feel like when you are relaxed?

Next, I take a moment to notice
what is happening **inside** of me.

I can notice what I am thinking.

(Thoughts are words I say or pictures I see in my mind.)

Optional question: Would you like to share what you are thinking right now?

And I can notice how I am feeling.

(Feelings are what I notice in my body when I have an emotion.)

My feelings can be BIG or small.
Sometimes I even have more than
one feeling at a time.

Here are some of the feelings I have.

Check in with your body, and using the feelings chart on the next page,
point to what you are feeling right now. How do you know that's what you are feeling?
For older children, please see the expanded feelings chart in the back of the book.

Feelings Chart

Then I take a moment to notice
what is happening **around** me.

I can notice what I am seeing, hearing, touching, tasting, or smelling.

seeing

hearing

touching

tasting

smelling

Optional questions: What is happening around you right now? What is one thing you can see, hear, feel, taste, or smell right in this moment?

When I'm practicing mindfulness, I notice things in and around me in a special way: one at a time and like they are coming and going, just like cars driving by on the street.

I notice things just as they are in the moment, and I don't try to change them in any way.

Optional questions: Do you ever wish you could change anything in your moment? What would it be like if instead you took some time to just notice it?

I can be mindful anytime, anywhere, for a short amount of time or for a **loooong** time.

Optional question: When would be good times for you to practice mindfulness?

Mindfulness can help me remember that I am connected to everyone and everything.

And mindfulness can help me notice amazing things about myself and the world around me.

Optional question:
What is one amazing thing you can notice about yourself or the world right now?

Mindfulness is like my superpower. Practicing mindfulness can help me feel better when I am mad, sad, scared, and even when I am happy.

Or if I notice something in the moment that is scary or upsetting, mindfulness can also help me to stop and think clearly so I can know what to do next or get help.

Optional question: If you need help with something, who can you talk to?

Let's practice mindfulness now and see if we can put it all together!

First, stop and breathe.

Next, take a moment to notice your thoughts and feelings.

Last, take a moment to notice what's going on around you.

How did it go? How do you feel?

Sometimes our brains and bodies are
so busy and full that it can be hard to slow down.

That is okay! The more you practice
mindfulness, the easier it will be.

Optional question: What makes it hard for you to slow down?

I will keep practicing mindfulness every day.

(And so can you!)

Growing up is so much fun!

See you next time!

Mindfulness Meditation
for Children

Sometimes life is busy and sometimes it is slow,
But no matter where I am, there is a special trick I know.

I use my trick to help me feel peaceful and at ease.
I use it any time of day, however long I please.

First, I stop and belly breathe to slow my body down.
Then I notice thoughts and feelings and
what's happening all around.

Stop, breathe, and notice, that's all I have to do.
It can take some practice, but you can learn it too!

As I breathe and notice, I slowly start to see
A still, calm, and peaceful, very mindful me.

Caregiver Mindfulness Exercise

You can practice this simple breathing
exercise anytime, anywhere:

Take a moment to pause and focus on your breath.
Close your eyes and breathe deeply and slowly, in
through your nose and out through your mouth. Pay
attention to the way the breath feels as it enters your
nose and fills your lungs. As you exhale, notice the
sensation of the breath leaving your body, and try to
let go of any tension in your muscles. As you continue
to breathe in this way, focus on the following phrases:

"Breathing in, I am present."

"Breathing out, I relax."

Continue to breathe, and focus on these words
until you are ready or need to move on.
You can come back to your breath and this
exercise any time to make space to connect
with the moment and with yourself.

Expanded Feelings Chart

Joy

Happy   Excited   Silly   Peaceful   Content   Grateful

Empowerment

Brave   Proud   Confident   Curious

Fear

Scared   Worried   Nervous   Shy   Embarrased

Expanded Feelings Chart

Anger

Mad   Frustrated   Jealous   Disgusted

Sadness

Sad   Lonely   Hurt   Disappointed

Other feelings

Surprised   Bored   Tired   Confused   Ashamed   Guilty

Especially for Caregivers, Teachers, and Therapists

Dear Reader,

In our daily lives, autopilot can become an all-too-familiar companion. When we are caring for children in any capacity, and it sometimes seems like we are just trying to "get by," we often rely on mindlessness and disconnection to survive (especially in the early years!). **Mindfulness** is a practice that can truly transform and awaken the lives of caregivers, professionals, and children alike. It allows us to ground ourselves and children in the present and can inspire connection with, and gratitude for, others and anything that comes our way.

This book is not an all-encompassing guide to mindfulness but is intended to introduce mindfulness to children in a simple and developmentally appropriate way. Read this book often as a way to reinforce mindfulness practice and to promote physical and emotional awareness. Don't be worried if your child doesn't appear to pick it up right away. The real goal is to introduce, model, positively reinforce, and create a home or therapeutic environment that cultivates awareness and acceptance.

Though mindfulness is a lifelong practice, and this book just the beginning, I hope you will find this guide to be a welcome and helpful addition wherever you are on your mindfulness journey.

Warmest regards and happy practicing,

Andrea

*Tip: This book is about more than just learning mindfulness. Although you can begin by simply reading the text, you can gradually ask your child more open-ended questions to reinforce the development of emotional intelligence and awareness. Create your own questions, or use some or all of the suggested interactive prompts at the bottoms of the pages. These questions will help spark conversation and foster good attachment and communication about feelings and individuality. Even though children may not always have the answers, the questions will help them start thinking about the importance of these concepts.

What Is Mindfulness?

Defining Mindfulness

In his book, "Wherever You Go, There You Are", Jon Kabat-Zinn defines mindfulness as "paying attention in a particular way: on purpose, in the present moment, and nonjudgmentally." Mindfulness also often includes attempts to let go of any attachments we have to expectations or to desired outcomes in the moment, and it encourages us to live each new moment with curiosity and gratitude.

Defining Mindfulness for Children

In this book, mindfulness is defined on page 6 as "when I stop to pay attention to my body and my heart and when I notice things around me just as they are **right now**." Keeping the definition as simple as possible allows for a foundational understanding of this concept upon which to grow.

Common Types of Mindfulness

- **Informal mindfulness:** This is the type of mindfulness highlighted in this book. It involves simply being aware moment to moment throughout your day. You can practice informal mindfulness anytime, anywhere.

- **Formal meditation:** This type of mindfulness includes sitting for a period of time and inviting yourself to focus on internal thoughts or feelings or your external experience. Though all forms of mindfulness are beneficial, studies have shown that formal meditation often yields the most substantial and lasting mental health and neurological benefits.

- **Movement meditation:** This type of mindfulness involves the addition of movement. For example, yoga, tai chi, qigong, balance exercises, and walking.

- **Prayer:** This type of mindfulness provides a connection between formal meditation and spiritual exploration. This practice focuses on letting go of distractions to become more deeply connected with your spirituality.

Tips for Helping Children Learn Mindfulness

- **Create your own mindfulness practice:** There is quite a bit of evidence to suggest that learning happens subconsciously through reinforcement we receive in our social environment. Many experts suggest that mindfulness is best taught when mindfulness teachers regularly practice it themselves. Attempt to make it a priority to cultivate your own mindfulness practice, as this will naturally support the creation of a "mindful" social environment in which your child can absorb this skill more readily.

- **Let go of expectations:** While pictures in magazines or on the internet of children sitting quietly in lotus pose are appealing, the reality of practicing mindfulness, especially with young children, involves going with the flow. Children are naturally wired to be mindful and to fully immerse themselves in their experience, but they sometimes need more creative exercises to engage their active minds and bodies. If sitting meditations aren't working one moment, try mindful movement. (Walking or balance meditations are great for kids!) Attempt to meet your child wherever they are in the moment.

- **Simplify:** Especially with younger children, start small. This includes simplifying the overall definition of mindfulness, as well as the amount of time you practice and the exercises you choose. (This one is true for your child and for yourself!)

- **Use mindfulness language:** Create an environment where it becomes common to use language that supports a mindful headspace. Ideas for incorporating mindful language into your daily life include referencing any of the language used in this book, reinforcing the use of "feeling" statements or "I see, hear, smell, etc." statements, or simply describing your own experience to your child in any given moment.

- **Interpret:** Cultivating mindfulness within children often requires an adult to help bring clarity to the moment. Phrases like "You are feeling frustrated because you wish you could stay up later" or "You're feeling so mad that you hit your sister" can help bring awareness to internal and external experiences your child is having. Over time, your child will start to connect the dots on their own.

- **Be curious:** Children are naturally good at being curious, but adults have often lost this quality. Though it is easy to get caught up in routine, it can be helpful to gently remind ourselves that this very moment is unlike any other we have experienced in our lives. Being present and curious about whatever moment we are in allows us to fully enter the moment and to let go of being on autopilot.

- **Practice makes "permanent":** Mindfulness is a lifelong practice. The more we practice, the more it becomes ingrained in who we are. Don't strive for perfection, but work instead for consistency and acceptance.

- **Model:** Besides cultivating your own mindfulness practice, mindful parenting requires intentionally being in the moment without judgment. When difficult or stressful situations arise in parenting or elsewhere, practice being gentle with yourself and with your child. Model taking slow, deep breaths; taking a short break; and/or reminding yourself that this is a process that may take some time. Though it may not always seem like it, kids will benefit and learn from your ability to model how to calm your own body and regulate your emotions.

Author & Illustrator

Andrea Dorn, MSW, is a mom and licensed clinical social worker (LISW-CP) whose interest in mindfulness, behavioral, and attachment theories began in graduate school. Since that time, Andrea has worked to incorporate the benefits of mindfulness into every aspect of her life and frequently uses behavioral and attachment theories to guide her clinical practice. She has found these theories, especially mindfulness, to be truly effective in transforming lives. She has also found clear, consistent, and attachment-based behavioral modification techniques to be crucial to developing healthy and thriving young minds.

The Mindful Steps series was inspired after a year of major transitions in Andrea's life with two young children in tow. Andrea found there was a lack of non-fiction, single-step resources for helping her own strong-willed child navigate and know what to expect during these big transitions. In order to fill this gap, she became interested in writing children's books and has discovered a true passion for the entire writing and publishing process.

What does this mean for you? It means that not only is Andrea's work and writing guided by her clinical and mindfulness background, but also by the care she takes in parenting with positivity, intentionality, and connection. She is dedicated to helping young minds learn techniques for calming their bodies and processing changes.

Andrea currently works in South Carolina as a psychotherapist with adults and children of all ages. In her free time, Andrea enjoys spending time with her family (husband, two kiddos, and dog), traveling, writing, dancing, and making meaningful connections with others.

Connect with me! www.andreadorn.com and @mindfulstepsseries